This book is dedicated to Rebecca Conrad Richie. She often went by her nickname, "Becca." We always called her "Mom."

Our mother embodied the attributes of unconditional love. The day after her burial in January 2015, we were visited by a ladybug that stayed with us until we placed the ladybug on a rose above our mother's final resting place.

The Ladybug's Gift is a true story which reminded us of our mother's love and brought us peace and comfort when we needed it the most.

This book is for children of all ages written from the ladybug's point of view. The message is a reminder of the true power found in the greatest gift: Love.

Love is patient, love is kind. It does not envy, it does not boast, it is not proud. It does not dishonor others, it is not self-seeking, it is not easily angered, it keeps no record of wrongs. Love does not delight in evil but rejoices with the truth. It always protects, always trusts, always hopes, and always perseveres.

1 Corinthians 13: 4-7

First and foremost, we want to thank God, to whom all glory goes. During the five years we have worked on this book, we have truly felt His comfort and Grace.

We want to extend a special thanks to Ken Foster, Anna Caldwell, friends, family and countless acquaintances who encouraged, inspired, challenged and motivated us to complete The Ladybug's Gift.

Finally, we want to thank our wives, Michele and Martha and our children, Hannah, Luc, Kate and Simon. They have been a part of this journey, helping with illustration ideas and editing. They are always so excited to share stories of their personal ladybug visits

Next Chapter Publishing LLC
Inlet Beach, FL

Text and illustration copyright © 2018 by Chris & Ryan Richie
Library of Congress cataloging-in-publication data
Richie, Chris and Ryan, author
The Ladybug's Gift / by Chris and Ryan Richie: Illustrations by Sang Nyugen
The illustrations of this book were created using pencil sketches and digitally colored

ISBN: 978-1-7358342-1-4

Www.nextchapterpublishing.net
theladybugsgift.com

The Ladybug's Gift

By Chris and Ryan Richie

Next Chapter Publishing
Inlet Beach, FL

My
Little Ladybug

Come here, come here my little ladybug dear;
I have a message for all to hear.

Where once I was, I am no longer there;
But I still have something I need to share.

I am at peace and surrounded in love;
For I am with the one who once sent a dove.

Heaven received me with such lovely bells;
But it was before I could say all my farewells.

My loved ones are having such a hard time;
Your message my little ladybug, is that I am just fine.

They believe I am gone and no longer will thrive;
But my little ladybug, I have never been more alive.

Heaven is beautiful and full of grace;
And the Holy Spirit connects us, in every time and place.

I ask that you visit them and give them peace;
For I will watch over them until their time shall cease.

And until that time should come;
Remind them to live in Faith, Hope and Love.

Guardian Angels exist and on Earth, they abound;
For those who believe, we can always be found.

In birds, animals and even insects like you;
So, my little ladybug, let this always be true.

That whenever my loved ones see you near;
Our souls will connect and their focus will be clear.

Life is short and will be over all too fast;
So love one another and your memory will always last.

And when you are in the presence of others;
They will know a love just like their mothers.

My task is for you to be my messenger now;
There is no reason for you to bow.

You represent God's Guardian Angels wide;
An honor that I know you will carry with pride.

I send you forth, go now and delight;
Show others there is peace when you follow the light.

Hi there, my name is Becca.

Becca, the Ladybug.

I am small and red with little black dots on my body.

I have soft wings under my protective shell and delicate antennae on my head.

My favorite thing to do is to make people smile.

Do you want to hear a story that will make you smile?

My story begins when I first met a special group of friends.   Let me introduce you to them.....

This is Kate, the caterpillar. And Simon, the snail; over there is Luc, the bee. And her name is Hannah, the butterfly.

They were sharing stories about their special and unique gifts.

The Bee has the gift of Loyalty.
The Snail has the gift of Patience.

The Caterpillar has the gift of Faith.
And the butterfly has the gift of Joy.

They asked me about my gift.....

Oh no, I thought. All my new friends have a special gift. "I am sorry, but I do not have a gift."

Oh, but you do, said Kate, the caterpillar. We all have a special gift. That is what makes you unique. All you must do is be patient and have faith.

In God's time, you will find your own special gift.

"Okay, I sure hope so",
I said as I flew away.

I wondered, could what Kate the
caterpillar said be true?
Does everyone really have a
special gift?
What could my gift possibly be?

Just then I saw something shining in the sky.
It was beautiful and had glowing wings.

Could that be.....an Angel?

As I approached, I could see clearly I was in
the presence of something amazing.....

It was an Angel!

"Hello, my little ladybug," the Angel said to me.

She was so beautiful and gave me such great peace to be in her presence.

She asked me to help with a very special mission.

The Angel wanted me to help make her sons smile again.

"Of course, I said."

"Making people smile is what I love to do the most!"

I realized helping this angel was important and searching for my gift would wait.

As I started my search for the Angel's sons, I looked down and noticed three men who looked sad.

I flew down to get a closer look.

One of the them noticed me, scooped me up and raised me to his face.

I let out a nervous smile...and he smiled back.

I could see tears in his eyes and I didn't understand why. It made me feel sad.

I started to cry too. But then I realized my task from the angel was to make people happy, not sad.

"Well, isn't this amazing," said one of the men.

"What do you know," said another.

"Mom sure did love ladybugs."

"Could she be sending us a message?" Asked the oldest.

I suddenly understood.

The angel whom I had just met was the mother of these three men. They must be brothers.

As I continued to listen, I learned their mother had just gone to Heaven.

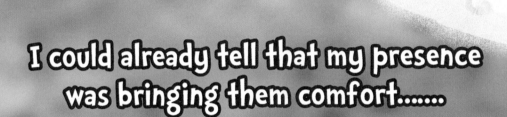

I could already tell that my presence
was bringing them comfort.......

One of them asked why I was out in the cold in the
middle of Winter?

Rare for a ladybug, they thought.

The brother with the fuzzy face searched for an answer
on his phone, and he started to read out loud.

I heard him say ladybugs are a sign of good luck and
that they carry a powerful message.

That made me feel special, and I wanted to hear more.

He said a ladybug's appearance brings an instant smile.

A smile that washes away worries.

That's me!

I beamed with pride and smiled so big, but then the man read something else which made them cry.

It made all of these strong men start to cry.

I felt terrible for a moment until I realized these were not tears of sadness. These were tears of Joy.

They had just read that the ladybug was named after the Virgin Mary, the mother of Jesus.

And that whoever is visited by a ladybug is reminded of a mother's love.

These men suddenly let go of their sadness and were overcome with comfort and peace.

The brothers thanked me for bringing them peace.

They said, "We Love you mom" and it was okay for me to go.

I thought I was helping the Angel, but the Angel was actually helping me!

At that very moment, I knew I had discovered my special gift that my bug buddies had talked about.

My gift is Peace!

I was so happy to have found my gift, but I was not ready to leave this family.

I watched their sadness turn into comfort and hope.

Their hearts swelled with love.

I joined them for a long car ride to their mothers resting place.

The longer I stayed, the more peaceful they became. They even started to smile!

We arrived at a place with beautiful flowers.

I knew that I had fulfilled my purpose and it was time to go.

I was placed next to a beautiful pink rose.

As we all said our goodbyes, I crawled into the rose to rest.

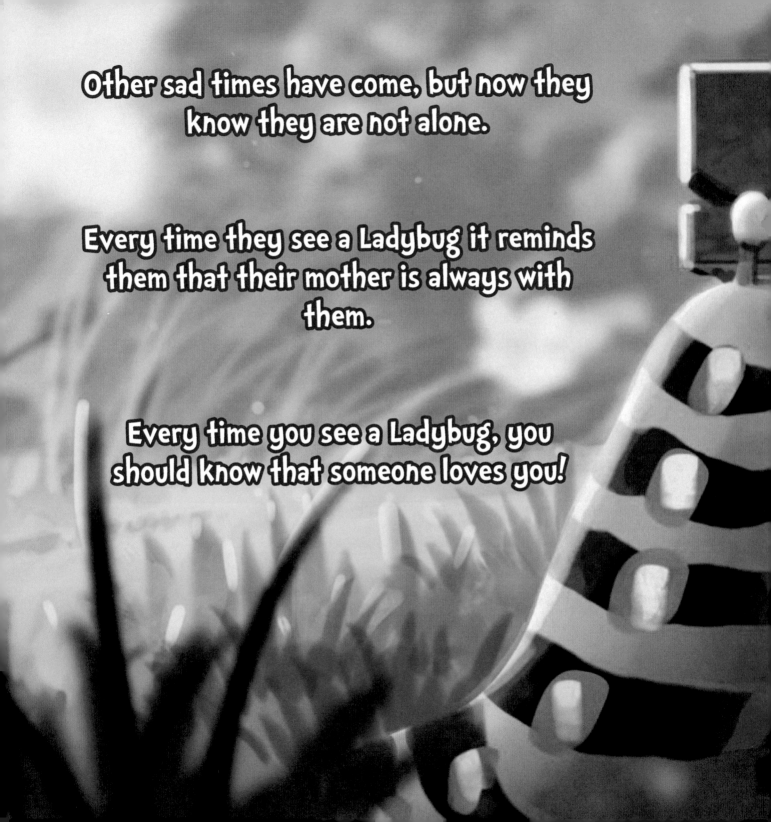

Other sad times have come, but now they know they are not alone.

Every time they see a Ladybug it reminds them that their mother is always with them.

Every time you see a Ladybug, you should know that someone loves you!

I hurried back to tell my bug buddies I had found my gift....
"Well hello Becca. We were just talking about you," said Hannah the butterfly.

I was so happy to see all of them and share with them my gift. But I was even more excited to hear about how they found their gifts.......

Yes, my lovely angel of grace;
I will do as you say and with great haste.

I see them grieving there below;
So I will go to them and ensure they know.

That their mother is alive in paradise;
And your message to them is profound, yet concise.

My very presence made them all smile;
Something they had not done in quite a while.

I remained with them all the way to your grave;
You would have been proud, for they were so brave.

I crawled onto a pink rose and bid them farewell;
There was nothing more I needed to tell.

They know you are with them and always will be;
You taught them in life, and now you teach them through me.

To let go and Let God control things from above;
And journey through life with Faith, Hope and Love.

Our mother passed away in January 2015 after a long battle with Multiple Sclerosis. Despite her illness, she always focused on making others happy and found ways to make people smile. Her actions demonstrated the true gift of unconditional love.

Rebecca "Becca" Conrad Richie was blessed with many talents. Among these talents was a creative mind and artistic skills. As a young adult, she created small stuffed animals she called bug buddies. Her FAVORITE was the ladybug.

The more we think of our mom, the more we realize that our mom lived her life, much like a ladybug. Whoever she encountered would simply smile and be happy. She could spread happiness and love in any setting.

Her legacy lives on through all who knew her and were touched by her love and strength in adversity. One week before passing away, she purchased ladybug bracelets for her granddaughters. She was wearing a matching bracelet when she was laid to rest. Three days before the ladybug story you just read (All of which truly happened), one of mom's granddaughter's painted this picture of a ladybug on a pink flower at a church activity. When we realized the uncanny resemblance of the ladybug on the pink rose, the painting which was created three days prior to our ladybug visit, and the ladybug bracelet she was last wearing, we could not help but to think of Divine Providence.

The Ladybug's Gift © is a true story which helped our family overcome the sorrow of losing our mother. The simple act of a ladybug's visit reminded us of the power of Faith, Hope and Love. The continual visit or sight of a ladybug lets us know our departed loved ones remain with us, in more ways than one.

Please join our Facebook community (theladybugsgift) and share your inspiring story.

And now these three remain: faith, hope and love. But the greatest of these is love.
1 Corinthians 13:13

Made in the USA
Middletown, DE
22 September 2021